Sun and Moon, Light and Dark

Tony Steven Williams

Sun and Moon, Light and Dark

Acknowledgements

My thanks to the editors of the following publications where some of the poems in this collection first appeared
(occasionally in different form):
Atlas Poetica (November issue, 2016); *In Response to Bridges* (SOM Poets occasional pamphlet 6, 2016); *Windfall, Australian Haiku*, Issue 4 (2016); *Swept Away* (SOM Poets occasional pamphlet 5, 2015); *Iconic Moon* (2015); *In Response to Triage* (SOM Poets occasional pamphlet 4, 2014); *Of angel's wing* (SOM Poets occasional pamphlet 3, 2013); *A Pocket Full of Spring Fever* (Writelink, 2010); *A Feast of Poetry 2009* (The Raglan Gallery, Cooma); *Prismatics* (Poets Union Anthology, 2008); *Bonzer!* (former ezine, 2003) and *Close Up & Far Away* (Central Coast Poets Inc., 2000)

for my wife

Sun and Moon, Light and Dark
ISBN 978 1 76041 608 9
Copyright © text Tony Steven Williams 2018
Cover: *Nebra Sky Disc* by Arlene Williams
Dated to 1600 BCE and discovered near Halle, Germany, in 1999, the Bronze Age Nebra sky disc is a bronze disc of approximately 30 centimetres diameter and 2 kilograms in weight. It has a blue-green patina and is inlaid with gold embossed symbols. These are generally thought to be a crescent moon, the sun (or perhaps a full moon), a boat, stars and two bands (one of which is missing).

First published 2018 by
GINNINDERRA PRESS
PO Box 3461 Port Adelaide 5015 Australia
www.ginninderrapress.com.au

Contents

Foreword	7
A tourist in the church of St Nicolai	9
Okavango morning	11
Okavango afternoon	12
Voice from a doorway	13
Man without fear	14
Stretching the amber	16
Don't you wish to be like them?	17
Wintry lament	19
Murphy's claw	20
lovers in arms	21
Beyond	23
Taken	24
Transition	25
Heart donor	26
Skin	27
Bone of contention	28
Band of honour	29
Jetty	31
Before security ruled the seas (1961)	33
The lake	34
Traffic light at Questacon	36
Namadgi peaks	37
Haiku	38
Autumn's gift	39
Bagman	40
Those IEDs just don't care	41
The two-finger cycle	43
Imaginary reality	44
The clock	46

Ode to a guitar	47
Old woman. Sad woman.	48
But she must let it go	49
The road ahead	51
Bittersweet	53
maintenance	54
The sound of one voice rapping	55
The last bushman	56
Cousins	58
Fairy Ring	59
The Ghost of Bounty Past	61
Orgasmic tennis	63
golden moments	65
I have a dream	66
Sun tan oil	69
slipstream ecstasy	70
Shadow in the wind	71
About the author	72

Foreword

When I first assembled this collection, I was worried by the diversity, which initially presented a problem for me in establishing a clear theme or a series of sections. On closer inspection, though, I realised that my poems alternate between light and dark and the various shades in between. This is not unlike our journey through life, where we constantly steer through the contrasting dimensions of sun and moon, bitterness and sweetness, feast and famine, steepness and gentleness, life and death, freedom and persecution, joy and sorrow; such are just a few of the dualities that dominate our human existence.

So here is my collection in all its variety, but organised into small clusters of like-minded pieces of meandering content such as narratives, travel, observations, moods, ekphrastic comments and outright fun. It represents poems I have written over several years with no specific final objective in mind, rather reflections on how life works from my perspective, a voyage through the light and the dark.

Tony Steven Williams

'Three things cannot long be hidden:
the sun, the moon and the truth.'

Confucius

A tourist in the church of St Nicolai

A tourist stares at Iron Age woman
whose veins still rise on twisted arms
leather brown, wrinkled
like the winter ditches crossing
the fens where she was born.

From tall windows
sunlight falls upon her body
sunk in oaken coffin
under perspex, on display.

In his hand I see a pamphlet –
I would like to touch him,
tell him what the words do not
but we float in different air, he and I…

I would like to tell him
of the scarlet-edged skin cape I wore
the day they came for me,
of my silver hair, running free
under a fine net bonnet
the day that I must die.

It has to be, they said,
your husband and your children gone,
and you a rich woman, with nothing to do
but mischief. Things have happened here,
and you, plotting in your solitude,
picking herbs, brewing schemes,
a bitter witch disturbing the gods.

I would like to tell my tourist
how they took me
to the acid bogs of Haraldskjaer,
pushed me into sticky peat
till my proud hair caught the slime
and swamp stench choked my soul.

How I screamed my innocence,
but they, deaf with fear,
placed great branches across
my breasts to hold me down,
clamped wooden crooks
about my elbows, knees,
lashed it all to stakes
driven forever into the mud
to stop my ghost from walking.
And how, alone, cramped with cold,
head pinned high, I faced angry gods
and a fading sun.

But my foolish people, my fearful people,
did you not know?
This spirit rose free that night
to walk the towns and fields of Jutland
these past two thousand years.

This poem is dedicated to the spirit of the Iron-age woman whose body lies in a coffin in the church of St Nicolai, Vejle, Denmark. Her corpse was originally dug up by workmen in 1835 in Juthe Fen, Central Jutland, on the ancient estate of Haraldskjaer. The cold, anaerobic, acid waters of the peat bog were responsible for

Okavango morning

Mid this morning
we drifted low in our *mokoros*
wooden hulls parting banks of high channel reed
jacanas dancing on lily pads.
A Nile crocodile slid under the water
invisible beneath its slow wake of bubbles.

The old soft-eyed Botswanan poler at our stern
never spoke. Wrapped in quiet dignity, he stood
on the edge of an immense generation
rift from the loud shirts and voices
of his comrades, their poles tilting against
the close green and brown horizon like the lances of a new order.

---

preserving so much of her, in common with many other 'bog bodies' for which Scandinavia is famous. From the scant evidence surrounding her death, it is reasonable to conclude she was killed violently, probably for sacrifice or punishment.

Okavango afternoon

Now we fight this bushfire
pulling whatever we can over nose and mouth
beating the flames with bundles of khaki bush.

Was it campers
not dousing their fire properly?
Or a careless cigarette? And what about yesterday's
mysterious meeting of the villagers and their chief –
had they concocted a scheme to discourage the tourist?
Striking over poling rates? Fire in their bellies?

The breeze is in our favour.
We back burn the grass close to our camp
and watch it catch and spark
catching two *mokoros* in a pyrotechnic shower.

The main front can't touch us now.
Black, scratched, overheated,
we return to camp
past a smouldering stubble of char.

Raw power and unease
are everywhere. Night air moves fast
through the brief twilight, its coolness
carries a jackal's howl
the eerie wail of a fish eagle.

I can't help wondering
if Africa ever sleeps
if Africa ever rests.

Voice from a doorway

The alleyways are tight, the air a hot towel,
bars on the windows, the smell of dry rot,
a place to move quickly, no place to dwell.

A voice from a doorway, a low, youthful wail;
I imagine her crouched, tucked into a knot
in that alleyway tight, the air a hot towel.

I pause, not wanting to pass, wishing a veil
on that head between hands, eyes staring in shock
in that place to move quickly, never to dwell.

Haunted and broken, the voice starts to fail
from that doorway, that hole in the rock,
in that alleyway tight, the air a hot towel.

Then silence at last. I take up my trail
averting my gaze, not wishing to mock,
in a place to move quickly, no place to dwell.

Softer now, quieter, somehow less frail,
I loosen my collar, hurry my walk.
The alleyways are tight, the air a hot towel,
a place to move quickly, no place to dwell.

Man without fear

High season. Lowering sun over Piazza di San Marco.
Floods of tourists decant from *vaporetti*,
chattering and crosshatching the trachyte floor edge to edge.
Waiters bend and skitter around the colonnades
of the great coffee houses – Quadri, Florian, Laverna.
Trays stick to sky-raised palms like a juggler's trick,
toting expensive drinks for people-watching as much as taste.
And those true masters of the square, the pigeons,
clutter above and below and all parts other,
putting the gaps, shoulder-riding.

We see an artist: Bavarian hat, Rose Madder feather,
Titanium-white tee quartered by Venetian red – what else!
Braces hold up indanthrene-blue shorts over burnt-umber legs.
Insouciant hands brush…pause…scrape…pause.
His eyes glitter sharper than an auctioneer's
as the reserve is shattered.
He angles back to compare the Torre dell'Orologio
to the north with its baby sister on canvas.
It must be just so:
– the Moors striking the hour on the great bell,
– the Lion, the copper Virgin and Child, the Zodiac.

Humankind, pigeonkind everywhere,
but as ants splitting ranks around a shrub
they leave inviolate his respectful space.
People stop and chat or peer, but nobody invades.
Even the pigeons do not intrude;
perhaps the odour of oil is not their passion.

We turn to each other:
Damn it! He is so good!
Painting in this place with all these people…
He is a man without fear!
Such a man would be here to work, we think,
come hell or *acqua alta*,*
come ten thousand critics or ten.

*acqua alta: high water

Stretching the amber

Why is life so complicated? So obligated?
So predicated? So overweighted?
A strident ringtone disrupts a patch
of conversation, a bus to catch,
a meeting to meet, an important fax,
a birthday missed (those deadlines can be such a drag),
a coffee cold and lonely, a half-dead fag.

Everything so on the spot,
present and future dot to dot,
even the past, if it suits us to,
can be reinvented with a lie or two
to snug in better with our whole-of-life review
where even a toilet stop is no longer a convenience
but rather…an *in*convenience, a hindrance, a grievance,
where sky and trees are but pleasant blurs
between our swift arrivals and swifter departures.

Life is uphill. Against the wind. A wearisome wart.
Life is a project plan. Life is an airport.
Wouldn't it be grand, a wonderful sport,
to stretch the amber between the red and the green,
to pause, reflect, to dream the dream,
to feel the grit beneath our feet, our cheeks turned to the rain,
to break that bloody airline schedule every now and again?

We really must find the space
to do this worthy thing, to break the pace,
untweet the tweet, unface the book,
disrupt the flow, blot the page, untie the lace;

when we have a moment to spare, of course,
when it's not so busy – maybe *after* the divorce.

Don't you wish to be like them?

So Yves Saint Laurent, so Benetton, so Dior, *je t'adore*!

They dine so impossibly fine, those holy hunks,
those divas divine. With shimmering sheath
and flawless teeth they shake it loose
in class caboose. So grand they stand
in their couture groups; in Paris, New York,
London and Milan.

Like brilliant rainbows dancing
in the mist above the waterfall,
they beam at us from glossy mags and daily rags;
the sweet dollar-rich smell of Chanel
lifts from the page and pulls us under.

– It's all about whom has slept with whom,
and who else is in the room,
and who has caught the casino bug,
and who is sinking too much port,
and who is chasing the dragon,
and who is drying out,
and whose wonder diet just everyone
should be trying out –

Daaarling!

Don't you wish to be like them?
To sample a swish of eau de celeb?
To strut the shoes and flash the hat?
To flesh the dress, to walk the suit, and all of that?
The Gucchi watch? The Ferrari car?
The reef of pearls? Lacroix?

But the dream's a dream, the waterfall's too high;
wash'n'wear on the *derrière* doesn't quite
compare with an off-the-shoulder Armani gown
on the wife of a mega-millionaire.

Wintry lament

one Christmas in the UK

Birds have flown, leaves have blown, I'm all alone.
Sleet, rain and mizzle, no warmth in the ground.
Gale, hail and drizzle, I'm chilled to the bone.
Wherever I look, no sun to be found.

No feeling in toes, a line of stiff clothes.
Car bogged in the snow, I can't make it start.
Ice on the porch, no torch, fell on my nose.
Shiver and quiver, it's bad for the heart.

Mittens, scarf, vest; balaclava on head.
Heating bills high and the mercury's low.
If not for Santa, I'd go off my head.
Oh bummer! Where's summer? Where did it go?

Murphy's claw

When the day is done and I am done,
and all is calm and put away...

When the feet are up,
dinner's down, cat's fed, kids to bed,
partner's off on his boys' night out,
a TV channel of my choosing,
a glowing red in my hand,
so soothing...

Yes, when all these things are set,
and my frazzled mind and aching bod
fold and flop
deep, so deep,
delicious deep,
snug, so snug,
in my fingertip-controlled recliner pod,

then it surely follows,
no doubt at all,
(and this the one night in the weary week
to relax and call one's own),
that Murphy's law will bind
its heavy claw around my neck

and visitors will call...

lovers in arms

the air
between
them
dry
tongue-thick
sirocco-fierce
superheated
fat-full
vacuous
slanderous

words
whip
break
slash
plunge

masks
heave
knot
scorn
threaten

eyeballs posture
dragon fire is thrown
across a table
of half-eaten cereal
& untouched coffees

then
      silence
              golden silence

arms curve
mouths meet
tears twine

contrition
forgiveness
generosity
bonhomie

whys and wherefores examined
judgements pronounced
points awarded
egos groomed
treaties drawn

the air
between them
preternaturally
bright & clear

cool change at last.

Beyond

On the edge he stands
high on the great bridge
arms wide
fingers touching steel pillars that cut the night
        into a sequence of stars.

He is a giant –
        an Andes Christ
                outfacing the moon…
Until
the sharp cough of a waterbird
        reminds him of why he is here.

For the first time he looks down.

There is something in the curve of the dark river
        that brings her back.

Brings back tears
        that cool to the stir of a climbing breeze.

He lets go
drops through cones of light
and wonders
if afterwards
his spirit will soar
above the glitter of the sky.

Taken

I'm dreaming of the hangman. The scene runs before me like a B-grade movie, my innermost thoughts dictating. Two prisoners in a cell-like space; one to be hanged, one to be spared. The executioner, a hazy individual dressed in grey, leads me to the gallows, while the other man looks on, his face scratched with relief, but there's also guilt, compassion and despair.

I'm saying *it's not fair* as my dream eyes watch me twist against the hangman's powerful arms. The white hood drops about my head, a closing shutter on my life. Never again will I know oven winds from the desert, cold sleeting rain, the crack and smell of a bushfire, the taste of hot Thai curry, the salt and surge of the sea, the touches and odours of love. Never again.

The hangman pulls down the noose; its coarseness irritates the skin of my neck.

And I'm wondering…how much will it hurt? How long will it take? Oh, this dream is all too fast, all too real; I'm not ready, so much living still to do.

And I'm wondering…will I wake again?

is this how it is
for those who die too soon
no reason, no crime
a fault in the camera
images lost

Transition

Fog lights throw amber streaks
onto a canvas of monochrome;
a sweating cloud has touched the earth.

No wind disturbs this dark, distasteful air.
A departing raven's question
cuts and carries the saturated haze.

I find a bench and sit. There was another, once,
who would have sat with me.

I shall wait, as she has taught me to wait,
for steam to rise from sidewalks in silver sleeves
under a warmer sun, a bluer sky.

Heart donor

I gave my heart away in Malta
let it gladly go, let it jiggle free
on the heavy-breathing harbour air
watched it vanish with crimson sigh
end over end, ventricles over atria

to a girl in a bar in Senglea.

Skin

They say skin is a single organ.

It shapes us, gives us meaning,
a visual presence: *This is who I am*!

So…
when you touch my skin
please know that under the wicked tip
of your finger
you touch the whole of me.

Bone of contention

That old bone
that hard old meatless bone.

Destroy that bone
fracture that fractious bone
baste and waste that bone
masticate, devastate and annihilate
splinter and crunch it
mash, squash and munch it.

Dethrone that bone.
Debone that bloody bone.

For if you don't…
as sun must turn to rain
and back again
that cantankerous old canker bone
that contentious old rancour bone
will still be there
between us
until there is no need for us.

So as that bone is your bone
not my bone
then do your stuff
because I've had quite enough.

And take your bone with you.

Band of honour

'Still there,' I frown
as we look down
at the gold ring
(diamond-studded partner
gone, thank God, but even so!)

'It's been two years
since you and Pete…'

(A pause. A gentle smile.)

'Perhaps to keep the hordes away?
Not ready yet to join the fray?'

'You're partly right.'

(She polishes the ring
with thumb and finger
till it shines, a genie's lamp
under her green, bright eyes.)

'Don't you remember when
we were at school? At uni?
I spoke nonstop of marriage,
kids, a house. It was my great dream,
my way of measuring success.'

'Yet your marriage was a fiasco.
And kids? Well they're not feasible
since Pete…'

(Her green, bright eyes flicker, cloud,
then clear – mist rising under sun.)

'Believe it or not, I am happy.
I own my home. I carry
some peace, some comfort
along with the detritus. Besides,
I have this ring, and,'

(she lifts her head,
almost apologetic,
but also proud)

'I have an ex.'

Jetty

Giant centipede
straddling the shallows
nosing gently
into blue infinity
barnacle socks pulled up
sharp to the tidemark.

From your hip hop
hot decks, boys bomb
(*spla-ooooosh*)
returning by ladder
under the No Diving sign
hair dripping with joy.

Lazy lines fall from
patient rods
burley, sinker, hooks
bait, lure and knife
landing net (you never know)
flask, tinnies, BLT.

On the dry, coarse sand
beneath your belly
it's cool as a moonlight kiss.
Bikinis, towels, snorkels
emerald water, salt-stiff
wrack, ozone overdose.

Machinery and men
once used your back
lugging loads of wheat
to waiting ketches.
Now your task is a smile
to carry in my mind.

Before security ruled the seas (1961)

Hawsers drop from moorings. A joyful roar
from dockside throats; friendly, familial –
curious too; all heady from the fumes and thrills
of towering, sunlit superstructure, smoking funnel.

Shoulder-bouncing infants wave,
parents holler and whistle through closed hands,
children dance, scream, reddened lips clamped
around trilling trumpets. On the decks,
tourist and first, passengers, migrants (carnival-clad in attire
they would never wear at home) gesture feverishly,
eyes locked on their fan base in the crowd.

Now the horn's triple blast. Three notes of jubilation
lift to the pub on the hill where patrons, raising glasses
to salute or glasses to spy, winking knowingly,
say for the umpteenth time: That's where they
and their missus would like to be, on that cruise
to the Southern Sea (lottery permitting).

Wash divides hull and quay. Last kisses blown.
Coloured streamers thrown high into the sun
drape the ship in party mode,
or, falling short, surprise the black water.
Another longer blast. The great ship leaves the harbour,
outward bound, heading for ports and magic
destinations, heading for the edge of the world.

The lake

This poem is dedicated to all those who think Canberra lacks a soul. Canberrans will, of course, recognise the lake (Lake Burley Griffin) and have fun identifying the icons and natural elements.

And the lake spoke to the man and his daughter, standing hand in hand near the bridge by the spouting water. And the lake grew excited because maybe, just maybe – if she spoke loud enough, and clear enough – they might listen; for she felt such an urge to say this thing, not having spoken for some time now.

So the lake spoke, and for a few moments her surface crinkled and deckled (although the air was still).

Undulations of water, winking under the afternoon sun, heaved outwards from her centre slumping onto the shores beneath the royal mansion, bobbling under swans and cygnets in front of the tortured sculptures, slurping eerily through the reeds of the fenlands, whispering to the giant loop on the peninsula. The belled tower, sensing something, leaned from its island to hear more clearly, while bladers, cyclists and walkers paused, puzzled, under blue skies.

Yachts rocked on their moorings, dogs barked, portraits stared; even lovers, tangled wildflowers on the grassy banks, sat up and brushed themselves down. Echoes sank in the corridors of power as the Speaker forgot what he was about to say to the fighting factions below – and wondered if he were losing it; while, in the corridors of learning at the foot of the dark mountain, lectures faltered in the strange hiatus. And readers in the Greek Lady with the French windows raised their eyes from their pages and frowned.

What the lake said was: *I am your soul, I am your soul, I am your soul*, over and over, over and over, until the man and his daughter, disturbed by the spray, moved on, and the lake, wondering if anyone had heard, had understood, added once more: *I am your soul*, before calming to a dimpled sheen.

And the days passed as if nothing had ever been.

Traffic light at Questacon

The moon's face glows like a wise pearl owl
in deep-space indigo.

Under its curious silver gaze
the white bright castle
that bounced with experimental zeal
is resting. Playtime is over.
Young minds are sparked
with sexed-up science
but bottling a cloud
and playing your heartbeat on a drum
must wait until tomorrow.

Nearby stands a traffic light.

Imagine all those energy lines
cycling moods of red, green
and ambivalent amber
somehow connecting back
through infinite digital networks
to a nearby hill
where another white building stands
transmitting tricolour judgements
on how many scientists
a country needs.

At the time of writing, bottling a cloud and playing your heartbeat on a bass drum were activities at Questacon, Canberra, an institution presenting fun science activities for all.

Namadgi peaks

the rhythm of pulsing boots
muffled by tussocks
the track soft and quick
but memories of huff and puff through
mountain gum and silver wattle
still held in aching calves

they talk with an easy banter
loose limbs loping under
a chameleon sky
jackets sleeved about waists
the air, cool and pungent
drips with eucalypt

pinched faces meet
the pure, hard wind of the uplands
fast clouds drag shadows
across a blur of bush
a circle of blue peaks
a bowl in which to dip the soul

Haiku

bluebells quivering
mountain gum, silver wattle
shade broken glass

Autumn's gift

When each gust shakes past days of glory
from my thinning branches,
will you recall my beauty?

When my russet rustling fades, and you
hear the creak of deathly tracery,
will you mourn my passing?

When you shuffle through crackle-soft litter,
raking leaves high to clear the sward,
will you foresee my resurrection?

When you scoop my golden memories
into large and coloured plastic bags,
will you sense their life force?

When you enrich your garden loam
with my grand gift of rebirth,
will you remember me?

When your flowers erupt in spring
and I live anew with fresh green splendour,
will you come and thank me?

Bagman

Bearded, ponderous, bowed,
the man of bags lumbers a lonely line
along the sidewalk through the crowd.
His eyes bolt hard to a vanishing
point on a strange, private horizon.
Two columns of square and shining
plastic bags hang from his shoulders
like ammunition pouches. No slanting
glance does he spare for passing shoppers
who halt with frightened pity, keeping
at a space, then in their guilt turn subtle feet
away from dampened, night-creased clothes.

Those IEDs just don't care

A response to paintings by Karen Bailey, a volunteer appointed military artist with the Canadian military forces in the Role 3 Hospital, Kandahar Air Field, Afghanistan (2007).

This world-class triage
deep in the desert
is no mirage.

Today our patients are civilians
Afghans, mostly
IED* victims, mostly
(their names little mentioned
in global dispatches).

Oh, those IEDs just don't care.

They are as brutal
as the desperate landscape
but with none of its honesty, none of its beauty
– with IEDs, there is no cooling breeze
from the Hindu Kush at dusk.

An IED takes away
with blind fair-mindedness
two arms and a leg
an eye, a jaw
– even genitals are fair prey.

* IED: improvised explosive device

IEDs are sneaky
hiding any place
buried beneath the sand
strapped to a donkey
– removing lives
with a random spray of nails and rocks.

Oh, those IEDs just don't care.

Civilians and soldiers alike
must not step out of line
in the world's most deadly minefield
– leaving parents, siblings, friends
weeping, keening, shoulder-locked
in bent and ragged circles.

But inside Role 3
multinationals
doctors, surgeons, nurses, corpsmen
saving, not wasting
mending, not rending
cleaning, not claiming.

Because another of us
is lying there
needing our help.

The two-finger cycle

Two fingers: *An insult*
Two fingers: *A gun*
Two fingers: *A victory*
Two fingers: *Peace be with you, man*!

Oh, such two-finger games seem never out of vogue
spinning in the blood of generations
a rattling flash of carriages linking stations
in an eternal circular route
where the points never change.

Imaginary reality

For all you logically
inclined: Surely it is fair
to push that it is not rationally
possible to take the square
root of a negative number.
Yet clever Rafaello Bombelli,
an algebraist of Bologna
in Part Two of the 16th C,
was inspired to moot:
I can't see any reason why
we can't assume the square root
of -1 exists, and call it i.

Thus birthed a whole new
branch called complex math
(what other hue!)
founded on a leap of faith
where what is real
has a zero imaginary bit,
and what is not real
is based on i and assumed legit.
Is this a pen I have in hand?
Or is it a false creation?
Do I think, therefore I am?
Or am I i for Hell's damnation?

So if God exists, or doesn't,
(and if not, then like Rafaello
let's have label *i* as a posit);
and if, as theologians avow,
God is in all things,
and all things are in God,
then God is God and I and *i*
and I am God and I and *i*,
which finds me in an identity crisis,
drowning in a philosophers' stew,
asking my next question, which is:
Who the blazes are you?

The clock

There's a clock in my room with a mind of its own.
It ticks like a metronome for days at a time,
Then decides to go AWOL not working at all,
Just silently beautiful adorning my wall.

Then after a week, for what I can't fathom,
It'll start up again as if nothing had happened.
So I'll reset the hands and polish its frame
And tell it: *Don't you bloody fail me again.*

My hiding it away achieved nothing at all
'Cos I missed it looking so cool on my wall.
When I put it back up, hand on my heart,
The smile on its dial was as wide as a cart.

It's not the battery, it's not that it's old,
But simply a case of a mind of its own.
I'd like to kick it right over to Rome,
But it's a gift from my mum so best leave it alone.

Ode to a guitar

Oh, lonesome guitar…

Scratched and chipped
pearls long dropped from your elegant neck
broken strings sea urchin spines
you're shedding skin in this junky shop
fretting in a swill of musty paperbacks
sorrow hearting with yesteryear's CDs

Oh, lonesome guitar, daughter of loving hands…

The rhythm and soul of the Saturday night gig
still rings in the sound hole of your memory
but your beautiful master, he's gone away
all tongue and grovel to the chemical lord

Yes, you were sold for a song of fleeting euphoria
but remember how he cried when wired-in lines
slipped from the maelstrom of his mind
and the plectrum shivered in his grip?

Oh, lonesome guitar, you're dreaming…

Dreaming for a keen-eyed musician
to raise you up and love you with a sigh
dreaming of a luthier to Lazarus it all
dismantle, reassemble, shine up the maple
born-again strings, ice-cream clarity
merlot-at-the-bar warmth… The diva is back!

Old woman. Sad woman.

Old woman. Sad woman.
Soft leather bag and hardwood cane,
each holds a freckled hand in rein
and guides her down the limestone lane.

Old village. Sad village.
To Let, For Sale, adorn the glass.
A silent school without a class.
The churchyard sinks beneath the grass.

Old river. Sad river.
Where red gums shade the wooden piers
a little less these passing years
and ferries rust in salty tears.

Old woman. Sad woman.
She looks across the reeds and sees
her brown legs flash among the trees.
Oh, the youth and joy of memories!

But she must let it go

The time has come for her to go,
to pause no more, to break the flow
of twelve thousand morning memories
that queue behind her swollen eyes.

Her heels tip-tap through empty rooms
and memories fade and memories come,
the walls shine bright and the scent of paint
deletes the past, yet it starts again.

She shuts her eyes and dreams awhile
of times to weep, of times to smile,
of babies, pets and barbecues,
a husband gone at fifty-two.

Her children had been far from wrong.
– No longer swift, no longer strong.
– Alone, unsafe, the yard too big.
– A smaller place should do the trick!

But they, so young, how could they share
this pain, this ache, she has to bear?
Her plants, her life, her soul, her house,
would now belong to someone else.

The house it means so very much
but the time has come to let it go,
for life to flow, for life to flow,
the time has come to let it go.

She opens her eyes and looks around
those empty rooms devoid of sound;
then quickly, lest she look some more,
walks outside and locks the door.

The road ahead

The old man felt that he was in the way
that age and wisdom simply did not fizz
that pretty faces always won the day
that funky punk and glitzy ritzy biz
and boasting, rapping, clapping could not miss.
These surely were the only ways to score!
No sporting star, he said, nor techno-wiz
could ever lose to wrinkle-sticks of yore
whose shrunken frames each year crept closer to the floor.

His wife replied she did not comprehend
his cynic's view. She said that being young
was hard, that few could reach the race's end
where glory lay, where easy riches clung
to an elite. And what of those who strung
so far behind? It would be more than fair
she thought, if in some pause they found among
the clutter of their lives some senior there
to lend a shoulder, and to have the time to spare.

The old man pondered this and gave a grin.
He said that time to spare was not so great
for them so old. He thought her logic thin
that she should think they had a chance to rate
in modish times that could not contemplate
a life expectancy beyond the year
of forty-five. Alas, it was too late
to join the global play, to act as seer,
to strut about, with fading curtains dropping near.

She shook her head in mock despair; it all
came down to maths, she said. You try to guess
how long before you shuffle off your coil
(allow for wear and such unpleasantness),
convert the answer into hours (bit less,
perhaps, for naps). The end result would find
a healthy sum in which one could impress.
The old man laughed and waved defeat; his mind
a trifle lighter now, the road ahead more kind.

Bittersweet

Your voice no longer by my side
in fierce debate or tender play,
the echoes still linger inside my mind.

And often I yearn, when I unwind
in the over-still hours of dying day,
for your voice no longer by my side.

Yet awkward partners were you and I,
hanging together like glass shards and clay,
the echoes still linger inside my mind.

It's been a while, the river has dried,
how long I'll miss I cannot say
that voice no longer by my side,

and it's true my life is newly defined,
old jigsaw pieces falling away,
but echoes still linger inside my mind.

Was it binding love or doomed divide?
It's hard appraising our shadow play
for your voice is no longer by my side,
yet echoes still linger inside my mind.

maintenance

it's all about grids and lines
curves and circles
ways we intersect
those broken rhythms, discontinuities

how we hold it all together
best we can
to keep the crystal shining

The sound of one voice rapping

The raven
from his tree of loftiness
peered over the wide valley
and emoted a cadent sequence
of descending caws
across soft mists
and hard rocks.

On his broad and forked perch
he turned an ear to the emptiness
and caught the most pleasing rhythms
of a kindred corvid spirit.

Deep within his thick black ruff
hormones sang a progeny prayer
and thoughts sprang strong
for him to strut his aerobatic stuff
(soar upturned, perhaps, across the thermals
seize an insect on a banking turn).

That should turn her on!
Oh yeah! Oh ye-e-a-a-h! Oh y-a-a-a-a-h-h-h-h!

The raven
shiny-eyed sex slave
to his own echo
dropped from his tree of loftiness
and barrel-rolled the rift
to an imagined future.

The last bushman

Grab life by the throat,
the last bushman roars.
Beer bottle slams on bar,
boots kicking dust clouds
across the boards.

He tweaks my throat
between callous and thumb,
dramatising his point.

Then, clearly a man of gestures,
he pulls my head back,
rolls my Adam's apple,
a ball of clay under his ale-cooled palm.

Seize the moment, seize the day,
the last bushman roars,
bouncing, pulsing, eager as a pup,
hot breath whipping past me,
high wind in a desert storm.
Wake up to yerself, young man!
Grab life by the throat and
wring the bloody life out of it.

But, I reply,
straightening my dignity
adjusting my composure,
ignoring stares
that splinter the barroom haze
as hot sparks around an evening fire,
if I grab life by the throat
and wring the bloody life out of it,
won't I have killed life? Murdered it?
Won't I be back to where I started?
Sad and low? Full circle?

The last bushman stills.
His aura hovers and clings
like clouds of blowflies on rotting roadkill,
going nowhere, going everywhere.

He brings his stubbie up
to his cracked and stubbled face,
throws his wisdom back in a smirking gulp.

Eyes shining with opalescent glee,
he reaches for my jaw,
waggles it from side to side,
pushes my lips into a cartoon leer.
Ha! You strangle life, you kill it, but you live!
Don't you see? You live!

Cousins

Our man from Hawaii favoured our multi-
national faces with a wicked, winking eye.
Youse my cousins, he proclaimed to
our many tribes, pausing for emphasis.
Youse my rich *cousins*.

A standard tourist line for sure,
but it is said that *Homo sapiens* has been around
a scant 200,000 years upon the rind of Planet Earth;
not near enough (they say)
to diversify (genetically that is) –
and well short of the span when dinosaurs
ran things down here. It is also said
that you can talk to any soul
        from any walk
and assay far less than one percent (typically)
between your and their demographical,
multicultural, denominational, mitochondrial
DNA.

So, if it is indeed altogether true that tint
of skin has more to with melanin
than race, then we
(and our man from Hawaii)
are hominids all, out of Africa, cousins to the bone.

Fairy Ring

Into the slow night an ancient melody comes
farandole crisp in the rare and fragrant air.

Fallen leaves dance
to chants of mantric wisdom
in an obsolescent tongue.

A couple walk by,
scattering the leaves,
grumbling some about the way
the wind has spun where none there was before.

A nuisance plain enough, a pest,
they say, and turn to go indoors.

In and out of silvered shadows
around the dew-soaked grove,
a chain of faerie folk weaves and bops,
spruiking gossip in soprano couplets
up and down the line.

In particular is discussed
a curious trickery
in the back of every mind.

Something unworldly has passed –
imperceptibly familiar –
no more in touch or time
than a butterfly's passing flicker.

Moon-song voices lift
through star-hung night. Linking hands
shape a trancing circle about the likely spot,
to try to lure and trap that which is gone

and long forgot.

The Ghost of Bounty Past

It's Bounty Day on Norfolk Island, a day of celebration.
But it seems to me, as we lay bright wreaths
to honour our ancestors in Cemetery Bay,
that our smiles are strangely forced.

An alien, mottled greyness
has sullied the winter-blue sky;
a once-soft early morning breeze
flays costumes about our skin.

We place the last flowers in haste.

Black clouds choke the sun,
shadowed waves snap a staccato
against the legs of Kingston Jetty,
heavy drops begin to fall.

If this keeps up, we whimper,
running to our cars,
our picnic will be ruined.

Wait!
The voice is a shriek;
we stop.
Even as the rain lashes our bonnets, caps and capes,
we stop.

Old Thomas, local psychic, descendant
of Fletcher Christian and Royal Tahiti,
stands alone amid the gravestones.
A long forefinger points
to a huge thunderhead gleaming cold
and imperial over the Pacific.
I see you, Sir, he howls.

And indeed, there is something
in its shape; a Captain's hat atop a face,
the Ghost of Bounty Past.

Bounty Day (formerly Anniversary Day) on Norfolk Island is celebrated on 8 June each year. This is the tiny island's most important day, and commemorates the landing of the Pitcairn Islanders in 1856, the descendants of the Bounty mutineers.

Orgasmic tennis

Chunky, tightly muscled,
the grunter shushes
and slides, closes
across the red clay
in quick straight lines.
Businesslike, blue shorts, white polo.
Two gold studs concede
to the fashion stakes. A slash
of sunscreen over her nose.

Thumping slice, topspin, lob.
Back and forth, diagonals,
side to side; thunking
hard through the ball
as if to turn it inside out,
favouring the baseline
like a safety fence
in a high place on a windy day.

Courageous, focussed,
the groaner,
lissom, elegant,
sashays, shimmies, salsas
in a stunning one-piece dress.
Cochineal.
Sponsors' logos, matching headband,
baseball cap with ponytail pushing
through a hole in the back.

Bright loops of silver swing from her ears,
easy strokes dance from her strings.
Knowing her left-handed kick serve
bothers her opponent,
she floats in to volley, to smash,
mindful, afraid, of being passed,
but fearing more the blitzkrieg
on staying back.

At first, we giggled at the antiphonal
grunts and groans, one high, one low;
then, as the match built,
the two-note tune was
one hypnotic whole.

One set all. The match tight
as a clamp. High note
and low note stretching
the octaves, never yielding.

Propped up by clap and cheer,
they shine in sweat
and glorify the eye.

golden moments

when shadows touch and leaves
        float softly to the ground
when a firefly flickers in the night
        and the moon glides past a cloud

the gentleness of a moment
        swallowed in the din of day
might hold for just a single breath
        but precious all the same

that sudden flashing smile
        as an argument overheats
a hand that reaches out to tap
        a shoulder bent in grief

such golden moments shine
        those little things that matter
mortar gleaming between the bricks
        binding us together

I have a dream

after Martin Luther King

I have a dream
that one day all hotels, resorts and apartments
will rise into the sky and shadow equally every beach,
and if a beach shall lack sand,
then sand will be brought in from more abundant beaches
in vast quantities
so that all beaches are created equal.

I have a dream
that one day men and women will sit together
at the table of a five-star restaurant,
and they will gaze outwards through the window
over the sparkle of the saltwater blue lagoon
ablaze with joyful swimmers splashing under swaying palms;
and all will be happy in the knowledge
that a very fine natural history museum
has been created
just off the atrium
to display the former wildlife of the swamplands,
and to showcase our belief in public education
and ecotourism values.

I have a dream
that one day even the mightiest dunes,
sweltering desert-like under the heat of the sun,
will be liberated, and transformed into lush green golf courses
with oases of water hazards to provide magnificent setting
and challenge for our guests. And first-rate real estate
will surround these golf courses
where all residents can enjoy their well-earned
freedom to gaze upon such verdancy.

I have a dream
that all our children will one day walk hand in hand,
for they will not be judged by the colour of their skin
nor by the class of hotel in which they have stayed
on their latest vacation;
for there is room for all.

I have a dream
that one day every valley will be filled
with monument and accommodation,
every hill and mountain will be made low
to provide easy access for all,
and even the rough places will be made plain
so that guests do not unnecessarily stress their bodies,
which might cause civil lawsuits
and other undesirable side effects
of overexposure to wilderness.

Yes, I have a dream
that even the crooked places will be made straight,
that these will be called legitimate casinos,
and all flesh will visit them.
Here will the glory of the almighty dollar be revealed.
Here wheels will spin and cards will flush
freely, fairly, and without prejudice,
delivering the same slight but equal odds
to all punters
regardless of creed or ethnicity.

This is my hope, and this is my faith.

With this faith I will be able to hew a stone of hope
from a mountain of despair.
With this faith, I will be able to transform
our nation from a hotchpotch and sterile barrenness
to a glorious, synthetic symphony of fully functional high rise,
while at the same time contributing to my investment portfolio
a fair and dispassionate return,
so that I, too, as I approach the winter of my life,
can be free at last! Free at last!

Oh yes. I have a dream today.

Sun tan oil

Super-successful magnate, tapping on your laptop
in the razzle-dazzle of your mighty emporium
building mountains with your fingertips
parleying with the powerful, partying with the celebrated
have you spared a thought beyond the glitter?

Don't you remember that blurry world you once knew so well
when the wind clawed at your face? Yet you would drop
a note into the busker's bowl, your soul singing fierce
the earth heaving under your feet.

It was not so long ago.

Present and past divided by no more than the subtle tan
sitting fashionably upon your skin – easily removed
so that you could once again step into that uncertain sunlight
feel the pulse that defines us all.

There is so much good you could do
if you would just remember.

slipstream ecstasy

after *Breathe Sketches (1)* by Harriet Schwarzrock, from the
exhibition *Defining Moments* at the Canberra Glassworks, Kingston,
Canberra, 2017

pewter fish on a silver sea
slide under and over the moon pearl
water, twining and twinning
through shadow and light
wet skins glistening
in the slipstream ecstasy
of a passing vessel

Shadow in the wind

after *A Wind-beaten Tree,* Vincent van Gogh, oil on canvas, The Hague, 1883

Lonely tree slugging it out on burnt sienna
Under lemon-yellow skies
Ducking, twisting, swaying, going down
Going down, leaf by branch by root

Inglorious artist, unfamous, going down
Going down, brush stroke by brush stroke
Misunderstood, disturbed
His paintings like seeds blown far

About the author

Tony Steven Williams was born in Penzance (that's right, the one with the pirates!) and emigrated to Adelaide in 1961. Tony and his artist wife now live in Canberra. He is a short-fiction writer, poet and occasional songwriter/performer, with work published in anthologies, newspapers, print and online magazines, and broadcast on the radio. Tony is a member of the SOM (School of Music) Poets in Canberra, which is an ekphrastic group aiming to explore the relationship between poetry, music and other art forms.

www.ingramcontent.com/pod-product-compliance
Lightning Source LLC
Chambersburg PA
CBHW062153100526
44589CB00014B/1819